Mac Wellman
Awe

Mac Wellman

Ugly Duckling Presse, 2019

ISBN 978-1-946433-24-4
First Edition, First Printing, 2019 (1000 copies)

Ugly Duckling Presse
The Old American Can Factory
232 Third Street #E-303
Brooklyn, NY 11215
www.uglyducklingpresse.org

Distributed by
SPD/Small Press Distribution
Inpress Books (UK)
Raincoast Books (Canada) via Coach House Books

Cover design by Cassidy Batiz and Don't Look Now!
Typesetting by Lee Norton
The type is Marion and Walbaum Fraktur

Books printed offset and bound at McNaughton & Gunn
Covers and flyleaf from Neenah Paper, printed letterpress at UDP

The publication of this book was made possible, in part, by a grant from the
National Endowment for the Arts, by public funds from the New York City
Department of Cultural Affairs in partnership with the City Council, and
by the continued support of the New York State Council on the Arts.

Awe

Allow me anchore! ! I bring
down noth and carry awe.
Now, then, take this in!

1.

‚Awful, exact,
wanderingevileyed. An
æ, an a and a small
letter đ.
Moon the color of
Sayyid's blouse;
moon the color of
cracked wheat;
moon the color of a
mouse;
close to a far place,
close to what is
an episode of what's
next; that rests her
head on your shoulder;
you too, bone weary, an
accident
that unfolded, here, in

the night,
night-bloom forest of
glimmers,
as it determines the
shape of one
      hand
upon the other: breath
and a

an and a small letter
misspelled
as
an eth.

Awful we say, and we
mean to catch
by ears the moon;

yes it is an o and o rare

Gone going a and an æ
and *eth* and
W double you. Exact

is a line, open at one
end. Far
Wanderingevileyed,
exact, awful.

2.
ℐNothing works the way
he should;

~

empty, oh,
ere, an

not. A

landscape wayland
knows

way land, a
what
Z drive all the way clear
past

Awfulness of the of the
whole shebang: an
and a

old cat dragging his
sorry ass home.

3.
ℬe and a cause open to
to to the.

Listing all the.
The. Oh. The

Wait till what is more is.

đ thee

(Eths and thorns)
o
doubled u o
...

Terce and a quite;
Squurd,

Notowl,

Nought.

~

Down (skze(e)ekle-
shaped) blade drop on
the un

suspected; un

care, full, too, full ytilt
till an, er,
empty
crystal sheer to to, the,
ah, to the
tenth yworld just a an
apart, go

the

doomed đ

Thorn's worth rights the
till

afar, way, land, and

so: goldish maketh the
hair

gold, on her, glimmer'd
like

a double u shared initial
capital

all ajingle

pizzaz, a and know o

~

This u is the only it to
be writ here and ever
so.

So says an o I, lowered
by use

likened, licks

lykwa shroud der murd.
A

toe ...

Shouldness of shoes
aloft and a

tilt, driving the tongue,

tongue till she

Gapes. Stands there, s
p q r....

A say so and a revolve
blade

hung till to paint above

the head. The one of
mine I do not
see

—

Sole bum tired and how,
too.

...

Bug noise and an evilish

think

o or or a how to of the

so lovely trickle you

đ [thorn now –

with her white side and
a an;

(just maybe she is a go)

You can't spell the thing
aright
till
to a
cause of an.
Justification man o
a
an;

to the till All tup is
buffered on a
bias;

cake

walk walk right, no

rose;

walk in rows, each self
an
o,
an o, another yet, yet's:
o so a so and so so that
is how it is....

Solitudes, *Soledades.*

Reply, the.

Que nadia me veia.

Just as each is, is each
a so.

~

So
as a usual a, a followed
in
with

the,

sorriest swivel you ever
didst ever
supposed
to spoot. Spit. Sput.

(Spite). And the

æ

W'd, double wheel, the
third
a
square stair climber; my
o
tail full of burrs and
briar and the like;

old cat dragging his
sorry ass

home – the

...

đ [thorn]

4.
Ꮯake and it three of
two: Two
& 2 plus 2

Taliban the second one
too
(Divell number not ah
not to tell;

Hohl's systematic set of
holes;

Set County's

O Siren high way
through to the –
the,

ouch Mayfield to
Wayland's
bluish

eye;

[)]

~

Strait is the.

As an episode,
measured in loss of the.

Lilts, and flying

tufts of a hair (barely)
hair; behind the old cat

song's ago

of an, an indivisibility an

anthologized by a

opportune lily, iris and
purplish orchid
æ. Do not stay in a a
double
tooth
Time wand. Hold one
finger

just as jazz.

Thorn man by the blink
blast black wind
drawn into proper
design as a
forked hickory of twig
and no
other branch. The

đ ...

As she calls wind, Go
and be

——

So's skin and
transparency:

liquid light as a a an a
crystal,

as an amaze
meant
creature's habit of
talking in
tongues

can know nor know not
how
not to.

That is just the point of
the.

...

Two's did my time in,
sport.

~

Old cat odd moment
eyes her

reluctance

breakfast bare feet skirt
short and an

o the too

Eyebright;

đ and to to hear for the
first a

no
reply

Soledades. Not to not to
ynot. O
shush all up till the part
in and
an
eye swivel in the
darkening to ah see
a
the
an
a
moonish?

—

Like a wand ...

Moonish is and an o;

Nornish too;

Narthex undulatum.

Tuum. Tuas.

Puella perdida – o
perfect in all the a the
way land

Ways the....

5.
Old cat with bitten ears,
tassel, no
way
out to a, er, ah,
a
a
a
trip to Ticket Heights,
place plotted   on
a
a

a wire, old cat
sanctuary;
big mouse barn;
leaky roof, but
losts of lots of warm
soft hay;

oh, the too.

Blowing green off and
on to a
an

anvil, the
big sky corked good,
ensorcelled,
&
up to U, double U ...

(T)horn ethed

an O, perfectalil(l)ly.
ImPact fine, port

mind-mine in motion,
just

a saying so and so and
so.

Still awèd; in

a perfect circle of
pluses,   problematics,

Shifts all steered to a
right-handed   ding.

~

*... wanneer we echt on
wachen ...*

_____

Like a wand;

but,

A we annulled, cancelled
as the the   the
tree of rain invisible
tooth took
too
to upside and down she
did a
far flung fling a.

Sheerest fall of perfect
O's and an O
intact as
quite did on her criss
cross and
shoe lace leakier too.

Tall to the, O, teller's

H ...

What the rains tell is a
name
three nose;

A not; A an; A fine thing
toyed
till
it and all kind else is a
not.

~

(O and does a the AWE
is ...
coughing bug to, to her

Ear;

ourr

a and an đ [eth]

And an æ

~

Is as does did ...

Laughing bug ...

W and the

———————

W

Wand the flat so.

~

Is. Dross. Do. Bear the
well
the well; a an
o
...

đ

Action is an acting as
well as a to the to.

Stop listening to to to

not know
   the

Droor. Snur.
Sssnossoossi.

X....

Gladness as she is an it
to not to
   too.

Ah a an oldy K; a
ah
a an & an er
up
&
œ ...

~

Turn to Kiss Land

~

Arnica perdita

~

The

Nothing matters.
Nothing

...

One word among
three
three of the a a two and
an a
three

Dust Dioscuri

Dust of brothers, doubt
and in a

all in a

...

Did be done the. All of
an x, small one

done in bye bye.

√ of the matter
[weasel] – new wrinkle,
all
below
the the the
red zone, fair the, way's
land
if
denominator

~

O
makes wise men mad;

hope hop and and ythe
poor

a just an a

too touched to be
so
just

alone with and without
the

...

Shirtless few

darned

doubled and toyed as a

boy who knows;

who, who nose?

~

Zeke old furled thang
done dog just a, an

đ [thorn]

briar patch....

A
fickle feckle fuckle; a

jstorm of woeth; a

jdarknoon
yknown to not no, no,
no one but 1;o

That it (to it) does not
upon darkest earth

call the swindle
a soul. It is, it is, sure
not
That it is so

_____

as a wand,

Error measures the
shrine's tooth;

Each a missed the and
an o. Simple. Trilled
and

chittering high in her

old damn tree ...

Ark.

(Urk yrk ...

Like Yaark but not like
Yaark:

[   ] thornless

anti-ark;

anti-all-anti omnium. A
jaa

Driddle draddle polist
polishman
who
errs in the of the

North of Yaark; A
spiked ray, A
fiddle town,
for the polite end there
spiked
an
a self quite the same as
so
in an also

đ [eth erked])}

—

Spiked the old ygun.

Possible to not do the
bough
branch
stalk and dereliction of a
a
just a bud.

By nots knotted. Taken
a
hold

of, feary one. Fiercest
bride to
be
oh open to the.

Oh and the angriest not

one.
Not one too.

N
Dee
N done.

~

Is she a a a still eth'd
ung

Quoz, a an

æ, an

a double-you L

lovely-lost

Mnoo man of the

No none, no

one, and then some

~

A
Question hangeth er
and an
a

slight hand moves upon
the stone
catching
it
cool to the touch,
troubling

Silence, motionless, at
the end of a a
a
a
a
a, a

stick;

Hide in the hay apple's
green wonder
underneath the

Heart's fortelleze, a an

abolished.

No to none. Now not a
ever to
be
there, red scamperer,
by a

touchy

[a single ingle strand of
ineluctable]

lost like ... a hair;

For, Form follows not
Function it is

rather, the other way a
a˙

roundy ydone ...

That is just ythat
precisely:

An
Arp of the sprocken
word, dizzled

under the inpropriety

Lame. Mighty. Lame.
Mighty,

One eye too many man.
For

What is the name of
that healing
emeraldish

stick thing? Go and ...
did it ...

Poison
the well; a an

...

đ [thorn ... still

To, to not too; to ope
the spill and
give
cause to what guesses
to go not
too fast in the.

In the acceleration of
nearly identical pictures

All of the same face, but
assumed not.
To allow
touches

in a little hot room, with
one little
hot window, no cat,
but a precious green
(set of) stairs, so.

~

In calculus consumed,
and a
suddened
why
who where are all the?

A pointless question
concerning
the
Sky's whereabout in the
in the

in the

in the in the in the inly's
inch
so just
be....

Stop thinking this, being
Moon that.

No hat so.

æ, ash, ashes all over
my face

...

Perdida, a place left

over by, and and one is

outside the

the, the

√

path of the. Both

the goths and moths are
as

đ |eth

to a pointless thorny, of

as, the

Moral Absolutist who a
an who
rocks
all vastest is

bourne; o wicked one....

Rocks (rock on!) ...

~

Point to a a a squarepoint-
speculate

all possible starts

'Sport'; the old and an
awe, up and
overthrown;
surface tension
surmounted

by a sac of furr

Ring-merism &
orthogenetic

sports. Shoes

growing other bitters,

one of a soft

unheard by them of who

ys ofttimes, grayeyed
slow to speech

if the messages
yunkindly,

'snip, or of a walk there
in
sheer summer's foot,
heat upon

the, o, the

foot pad – these
Big Cat Feet.

Note to the Unwary:

Innocence is no not

Unreal.

A
Thing has five aspects,
four
hid in
the
mitten a kitten hid in it
and id
on
the first day. Aer Are.

~

A splatter of splats &
splays
ac-
cording
to someone's
ydea of a an
and and a
sky, o,

đ ou,

monstrous & unkind.

For [eth] Doubt

gradually loses his door,
becomes
a
a, an
a
...

Small wit child, enraged
at what
falls
as if from a nothing sky;

not nothing knows

a

simply a....

An

out of work oval, wide
foot

.

Nothing to bring a name
to
on foot or on

no foot, a sparkle.

6 and 7.
airplane witch doth both
goth & moth

A
an O place in the in the
X
place
not to be a
name
less
than

spatter spatter splatter
a dis

p
lay at

æ
;
...
All for the sake of, say,

Old cat drags his sorry
ass home.

8.
New place now and new
the whole
allest
over
nation not;
until
now a viewed
L

lustration ...

Of a an

Panta Rei

Doxa

Luna & her

61 rayed solar opposite,
not a

not
a a a foot away, you
can too

touch the sunlight

as he passes through
you, all

to a an

inner radiance, radiants
quiet now

the whole damn hoopla

(A if as)

stirred with a stick

my old
hickory, not

to be something, but to
learn

to be able to pass long
to those
who

something of some
damn worth.

Some damn cat's

Sniff

sniffsneffsnyphphphph.
An L

to the
a
a
a joy stick place. Sky
on Yaarth

(O an ...

Earth will be air again,

Earth again air; the

not
a the

forever time.

...

The. Here. Most now.

~

Sudden up to to turn
and on a an

a
alone, proceed, with
longish tufted
ears;

squerve

not to not know

how, how
to.

(Drat)

~

Iff (if and only if)

As it was, with iff with
quick little
P(priest)riesting
S
teps

,
all the way the to a

(iff)

Moon.

Not another one one
one a

one who;

is an awe –

A(lizzy)W and 7 ears;

count 'em

~

All on a chilly moon's
horn of a

the
est
silvery documenta; no

no larger
than
a an eye to ah to touch
the
the estest

bringer of a stars'

motion weed and water

singer,

likened to a new clink

All the gravest

to talk to; to talk to

and not to be

~

...

That is the.

Yquestion?

W?
æ
And the at to be so soon
so on
&
all the
at rest
all the

rest

11 and 12 August this
summertime 2006

Too daze

hard
to be thorough to all
else it tis.

Why now
and why
not now? Give it to to
the

She call

a

no to no one now.
Eared
no
nowth ...

Burro. Burros in a
Timocratic tin ear

pencil unsharpener

to no death door

~

A
black-eyed Susan
blossom in a the
Wee
blueglass bottle
enough
now on the
œ
no
đ [thorn];

Where is the

?

The. The. The.

A trystero a system.
Adhesion all erp
to a novelty; an ynot

no potsage for no non
delivery

and an o;

empty as the the (the)
day
is long.

Onliest eth
person on
off on a an if iffs

cubic cloud unglow
yredly &

by the

Motion shall (s)he be
known

o
crye ...

Set off a and the, the
stick

as(k)
To question the.

What is who. Who is
what.

Old cat: Wonder why.

~

...

Old cat: Wonder ynot
why?

Titan Arum

sniggled, squonked and
smutch'd

who
is what
and
therefore a a a

Why (Y)?

What is what's's more
than the
what in what,
thinks old cat, uncoiling
tail(!)

Sad excuse for a.

On a.

Smallest thing, a dust of
all
non
deliveries;

devilish, dervish, evilish

spools, tops, toys on a
the of
you
who do
dust to dust
are ydone;

o saddest corpse flower
do not

...

(æ)

ydone did to a nope
nothing (for nought).

Spin, *darwish*, spin.

~

On a
la
la, lilt; an a; an an; la la
–

a a a

a, a

tilt. To be the, so.

And so a a aa thing
thought so,

a a a

A. A. A. (honk)

clean sweep of all
thorns;

đ ;

All to type drawn as by
the.
The thirst of an origin

Awe is an; o

other than she who is
who

some darn other.

Niddle. Noddle.

Stare, starling, stare.

~

on and an
on the either side of my
head

as at the.

đ [eth)

~

Nonce word none. Just

an ape on a a a, yrp, a
chain.
Glassed

Open, eye! See the all,
as
as asterisked,

to come to a the of
thought

empty
of no selfish;

O Mahbub: O the
utterness of all ends

.

(And what shall take the
air of him?)

A the sixth thing qualia
does
doth

And to the but yet not
to the.

And an a to the but yet
not to the.
And to the ultimost till
all the

Stilled
re
doth an ewer of ilkest
the.

~

As the dust of all doth
go
to
a silvery moment, just

a

an.

And, say, who? Whoth,
says so

(Is it? It is!)

Wickedest daring her he
to,
too.

Awful awfullest awf.
A an
too.

9.

ʽSibb hath too an oncet
for an Eye

rie (man)

let, too,

to squib, as does the
CryWolf
W;

noun times ydark and
foom
by;

too ghost an ghast in
fair parts
equally

to be all an

overendoubt.

...

~

đ [thorn]

Now you can pick up a
anything,

old old cat modulates
the y the boom:

Awf. Auk and
re
and
ytooted by nether
outcomes ...

Obsessed Gorp;

Loud Shoe Person; at

nixed
to be
an
X hope not till to a a a;

(overendoverandoubt)

a an ann ann(n)
ever
an old cat wonders at:

An awe.

9 (10?)
Teuffel mutt toffee
cat
zeroes a no
do
you do do you
have to er ah
have

a
a
a

~

; a an; a not
an

yslink and you just a
er a-

an accordion:

Menger Sponge

    [a picture of this]

Stiffle (zek [k] kily)
prickle.

Y. Yglinks. Us. A.

Usa ; a

a
thrumneedle
stack
blade
itch:
I
tchery ... [iffs]

~

...

Norpth; Sooth;

ð [thorn, eth]

and an æ;

pagethirtytwo: sdops.

~

.

~

[soledades]:

See their bright eyes as
they track

Some dang thing after
another
(or so quod the old cat)

10. (The REAL ten)
a scale is revealed of
heart & feather

a and a
merely a; an a;

so and so not. The

Too stopped on a a a

dime.

~

Skekels. Tip. Ske
[nickelz] kelzeckly. Tip.

~

For
sky too has a ribbon of
bright mice &

leathery moucherie; tilts

and lilts of fair feigning.

Neither does the dust
all
know;

scatter a wish till she
settle on a
prism, just as a poker

judge
just at pink's dawn,
eerie &

So as a

as a

a fennec's ear ...

𝔖

Straythecursive!

11.
'Elf ifs and und end set
of an a;
so
a
as a shuttle's loom;

breathe

eyes on a far point,
without a
clue to
who
is arrested and who can
be not;

a an of set end around
        and und if(f)'s elf
ish
so.
So that so an else parks
shelf at
Mister
Mooncake
foot;

So that so and so forks
a lifted tiff
to
a an ell;

All complete parsnip.
Senators

Smip and Rhikk appoint
me

the too Monsoor

Whip Wind lake break a
corner to

To a an.
Par(rrr)ied. Shelfed.
Veld. Consider a out
law
as well as the

To Do howled, loud,
aloud, beloud.

A prickle in the sunlit
field, there,
up
the old hay hill.

Mac's call;

braced for the
solo
solar divinity, ashrew
with

an electric bumps.

Mishe mishe;
mishmashed ...

Valerian to a v note

~

I can't use it anymore
[i.e. his tattered tail]

œ

'll

to a an ...

(To be continually in

awed

and

iffn it don't work, quod
the
double u'd crywolf,
don't (go and) fixit ...

Kapakapuk ...

3.8 lpf; 1.0 gpf:

American standard.

~

...

O, a
past all the futures;
past the al(l)l to and up
till all
if(f)s

reverse the recursion.
Apple
by
apple by apply
by

   the Moon the;

anew, anent the
scrabble time-

tune in, she's a double-
pinter

ism. Isis, if(f) –

afloat in foo, nights
feary
father
one, too

For
whose quaint peculiar

book
is mine?
Thine – [echo opines]

as of of this Forgot the
Pulley
'
s
loud
sing and dollies up there
a

considerable ydead
weight
drop
load of the mighty:

æ
,

ethed. An aweful frieze

circle squared a square
circled

no

perfect geometric;

anent the scrabble time
tune
in –
no cat noses knows the
moon's
butt so;
So goes the old cat,
alone
in
a winter squall....

Cat shadow shudders
snow
field

and above?

Nebula beyond all barn
hay.

Is a cat god sleeping at?

At Cat.

As a man speaks he
lies.

Squeaks.

[... squonks, squunks
...]

What goes, goes
(simply) not
wishing to;
adverse – an
alarum though twinned
in
the
moon bird's black hope
mirror.

Snaggle the.

Winter return awe's
favor

with
silent tips. Far away as

a pink

rosey roundness.

Old cat down by his
scratches.

Old cat so slewn;

a mind in muddle:

A tip on and as a to to
the tricks
        of aire's

o

~

O, a

~

Talk to till Awe is truly
tipped
by
nowt but
a glee;

I cannot thread the
needle, um;
I cannot dot the I,
thinks the
old cat, therefore what
am

...

Eye

...

(?)

!Do
Do not
Do not do either thorn
till
the
perpended

tale is addressed,
repaired.

Cat sings:

    I was did
drop my soul
    upon that
track he, I,
    did not did
what to do.

    Them trains

blast
over
hats
and all I

could not was
for that lost
soul of me.

But the
veriest light
split twofold
as the train
off and
closed up after.

All had
passed.
Yes.
Once
more

Closed up.
Old cat,
I, was
Glad
outcome had
not to fear.

Cat howls:

Bron ton
bron ton.

Bron ton
bron tonka ton.

Bron ton
bron ton tonka
ton.

Zeckle ton
ton tonka
zeck bron
ton!

12.
𝒩ebulinae:
beyond the dream
of the sleeping
god ...

~

An initial a;
a flo
ating squ
are ydarkeneth
the crie
as it he her thee
there fluted
apple cryst
al st
art up system initi
als
an awe; irps

~

Guess it cd have

been ysomething
important, but
eye guess it
wasn't;

perhaps an eth in
transit, perhaps
an

... œ ...

[thee – eth –
thorn?]

... œ ...

As
an old cat
gravitates till to
the
high
ball
state of low ball

quietus; go

and woeth to a to
away
to
to æ a

and to a gall
wherehesoever

drives the Pickle
Chief

so wood roars.

Quiet rights
what's upwrong
and
of dough.

~

Dough?

~

Dough.

Dodo.

...

!

~

13.
℘inging all the
letters of the
alphazetabet;
quiet

catanda, voiced &
unvoiced. A

error mendicant

old

cat rebus riddled,
rattled,

semi-tufted,
symmetrical

and

who

threading the
needle of
impossibility

doth repair thy
tail
tattered
o thingum. O,

o dodo tail, now
of genius:

An awe

a dodo dada tail
all hope
gone

All tails

"... in the hands
of the Allambys
..."

(Hope is gone):

Hope (poke,
nope?)

_____

_____

_____

Crap is such a
lovely word,
thinks

Old Mad Daddy
Cat rubbing his
muzzle
on
the
tip
of the
nozzle of a red,
rusty
a
er
a mad wall, erk,

ð [thorn

and out;

and if it comes to
hat,

just

get thy cat upon
thy shoulder,

saith the Lord, Go

and get thy cat
upon thy head.

Ovoid, because he
splits the Egg ...
Ovoid. And
an awe ethed
ð.

~

...

; as it doth

æ inches ah aha
he fear ward
way fear ward;
so,
so

earish

much twixt those
earish twos:

Forks face West,
an

odd oldy cat
ysurmises,

pilth and tilth.

{Pilpul, the tilth of
the of the
telk er telth;

;;;

~

...

}

Overland in the
high hay she
doth goth and
goes.

~

Mizzou, thinks an
an er elf
mussed

too till to an

æ is as a cat's
paw

đ

thorn. Of an off;
an offshoot,

un

undertook y
ystuck (Tuck's
crystal
...)

.

And so an on is
yquite an off,

an

an never

niversary of the
old cat's total
off....

~

14.
Old cat doth his
hurt foot all the

rain
houch they have
some
er
damn pretty, er

hen's teeth

hen pan

...

Go wide; gather
   more – treat
   the sorry ass
   &
   tail
   to a
(how much land?)

Treatest rare.
Nowt

trouble the with

an o o o
without such
disgrace of
ae tail

pad pad

old cat thinks:
    Could've
    been
    something of
an
er im
portance as an *ae*

thorned oh ouchy

least than around
then most longer
than
she'll be
more than my
battered
    eldish

o tale and

what
a
kick in the head
...

~

Look at at at that
at at that a that,
thinks Monsoor
Oldy Cat,
Sorry damn
excuse for a call it
ha. Ha, er, tail.

If(f)s abounding,
worse than
thorns:

đ [thorn:

after an
an *ae*; an 0

flattened out to
recall the (oh!)
The perfect, er,

Erp. Low

Lowly, *ae*. Minus
her W.

───────────

───────────

─────────

The Porism the,
fills what she
expands with-
its
if(f)s and a er a
thorn

of nots yroundly

woven;

soft as a feather
chair;

coaxed into the
the IF of being by
a blue night
's

curlicue'd hammer
link to

chop aright
solo,
done chopped and
waived, by doth
and goth both:

Slow boat goeth.

Hammered
dulcimer goeth.

Goth goeth.

And so is a quaver
to the too; to the
tune of

a single a

candle aced; so
the good fox

Bore the bad
shape of the, to
the.

~

đ the eth and
ether and ethest
of a a a *ae* a

dust-writing is in
awe of all

900 times to be
tuned X to the

as all of and off
and all If(f)s
escape
a

W

stone-whacked
and fall into

"... in the hands
of the Allambys
..."

More than once
more.

Old Cat: Get thy
cat upon thy
shoulder ...

An never ha ah
ah; aha. A word
says

such a tail teased
by Porism:

An ology of
morphs.
An ology of paths.
An ology of sorts.

And an

ology of torts
        an
ology of warts
        an
ology of fudge an
      d

        an
ology of all such
suchness

...

An ology of ones
and twos,
an ology of crystal
flakes,
an ology of nuts
and berries –

(Berries bird-eyed
bright)

– an
ology of dulled
and sharpened
    edges;
        an
ology of wrath
        an
ology of cries
        an
ology of laughter

an
ology of sneers
an
ology of fright
an
ology of dreams

an

ology of scratches

an ology of
hilarity

an ology of awe.

ae awed by *đ*
(thorn); *đ* (thorn)
awed by *ae*;

both done ethed,
ethered, ethiest;

Awe touched by

air's can
noodle;

Nutt's spray, an
never not to be
uttered
by a
lip, such a
loveliest lip
mouthed by a an
a an

Airy O; once –

Once more, an

never
outs
an other one once
and – yikes – an

Old cat drags his
sorry ass home.

fun last   ear nest

|then X

~

An o and an *ae* in
choral refrain
as
the concussion of
Watt does the
stop
ages doth too;

too too tooth and
a

scrunched up ear
flap –

all there is, that
that
is all there is
nowth.

ð |thorn|

...

~

Forth by a ah er a
brightest earthy
shine
     o and door
whack

daynights'
possum of played
out dreamily
mis
drawed dregs;

hopes of sheggs
and renegs of
drouth; an

annulled;

timed to misfire
all around the
and, eclipse, of
else not – nowt:

now 'tis a not
now....

~

"... lost without
you ..."
The.
Cannot be
spoken,
much
less to be said,
spoke.

The
sad.

~

Not a now thing;

but by ant, by an
a slow
plush
pockety pock of
soft slow feet and
not credible, crie
credible and

Snout Curious, an
ether

star, far far.

Far away through
nameless
mountains
thar.

———

Thorn thorned,
eth ethed – a
picture of this and
        of a

nowt:

(đ) đ as the, the
sputhering ywind
fearly foretells

(Call me Broken
Wheel)
An *ae* as an end
to all

If(f)s; as if the
only

Stood There,
there, at Stone
Mount's core,

a ...

a, a;

an a and a thing
apart.

As though a

hurt colossus –
patched part of
the

a, a;

a ... (an [Ann
Never];

Central
Mountain's stone
at

there, just a

stone

~

As if the horizon
were as simplex
as is the of a

Wand

_____
_____
_____

Lowest moonmorn
blazeth of
Magpie light
doth &,
ah, adest, be
a heads
off of, er, all the:

thou those
sheerest &

dumb best

daisy: chop,

chop – daisy not to
fear;

he done gone;

Old cat smiles a
wicked one and
an

never ace of a

torn tail. Ears are
like wise bitten
so,

so: Old Cat's
sorry tail.

~

o, an a

~

o, a;
enough of these,
shish you

magglepie;

peekaboo
tricksters ...

Blackened pot and
blackened tooth
and the

eth
is
adest to an odd

Spike, just an *ae*,
far off and far

Gone; gone thorn
(Ð

under a the an
understone and

under known, o

Old Black End,
self to a
streaming of
shelfish –

Shall the shell be
as to a night
drawer,
        Monsoor

X? X, thou ethed
&
so ...

Grown Feary to
thy

(S)tale....

~

All motorized
hummingbirds A
rise
&
gling ...

~

Wandering
evileyed and Wall
most more mere
most
apart
Dd
cat. You hoo
means

to an either down

tore down

Yi(a)ikkytty Yak
... The crick doth
not goth

a high hill for
nowt:

Old Cats does not
does not does not
comprehend
his tall-weed
his er

tatter for a

tail.

~

Wand if air o o ah
o an erp ...

Wand of wind lay
and ly and his

down, a thorn

omen did. A
bone abolished

....

~

Thinks: Old Cat,
mordant
one:
Only
Wood weasels
shall associate
with me, and
those of the

air – Magpies

(As a flourish of

pied silk,
animated);

these are the
answer
to
All's silent
reproach;

Even the
shadows, now,
squawk –

Now an
ae
thorned,

turns the tussle,
thus and so, into
an exact

invisibilitie....

O

the art of the
never-asked

Owl-question,
who is

the too-tormented
to
speak quiet, heal
what's

hurt whispers and
other less than,
ah,
an
O, an inert

hurt places, dumb
to speaking

than with a a (a)
a cry

the self

(That, which)

So like a whisper,
among the little
noises
at
a dawn

So light of wing
she can fly

As if on automatic

An an
annulled twice,
seen
no
more, like that
purple wild

flower w/o no
damn name nor

~

_____
_____
_____

O Wand, strike it
hard upon the,
the

The spurkle of a,
of a spurple snowf
lake
dzzle-dzzle
upon the
up
on the
dazzle dizzle;

so:

She stays

stays the

one rightful wrong
from an

eth

of confession of
toggles on the
upper

aer (o oldy
home!) Of ah, er,

a

a, a

stopped nap by
way of sleep

broke open

flower focus –

ignoted

like the idea of
the

permanent (not
eternal!)

Fall [Ð: eth

An o:

{Permanent (not
eternal!);

An awe

~

An if and

an
if (f) of all

the(se)

hidden places
whose all the o an
outermost

reach

of the noise nose

about; friendly

(O *ae* merest spot
of talk dat

dat
dat
dat

spot dat, dat
spot....

~

{An Old Cat Ball

battered or blown
by?

Curious the
bat;

one, er
eerie   (...
)

Erp, consider an
apple, the, small
tart;

wonders ...

A hopeless
tattered
tail, and

Wonders (an *ae*
ethed Ð;

considers the
dead

BALL

a place to
circumambulate,
fall off of
and
do the drop

)

Wonders as they
do
Oldy
Cat:

Why not ydrag
the whole mess
home only only
hwere is ythat?}

Does an

Oldy homage to a
Ball;

another gone cat;

19 June

a
day delivered....

Wand

says it is a.

Photo.

Photo total of
nowts.

Er, er, erp.

Phlogistical

Kludge.

_____

_____

_____

Awfulness doth:

Nix
A all pix
in
the name

of Ah

Ð [eths and if(f)s

~

Too too to drop
from
a
an,
almost a

a

~

a
a, a
a, er
an

a;
a

~

masked, as
asked, and

an

announced as a
wait

a
a

a
weight dropped

from a

Ball to dot

call me   (N
                  o
                 no
                 t,
                 er
                 p)

Dot now, Ball

(One whose
weight has).
Quite the
drop

old Devil Shine!

A

wait till now, this
hotness
who has an

~

till toppled
too

that is,

an otherness
weight
to drop too

dot, dot, dot ...

...

Some one makes
a prayer for Ball

Roll the, the,

as we doth we
goth –

purple flowerlets
hide from Mowers
we

We who ball and
an

ae plus the you,
doubled must

thorn, not moth;
a

a, a

Pause for Ball.

~

All anathemas are
occurred

in the
pattern. Old

cat grins a
crookedally....

Noth, he reasons,
doth;

purple pansy
plush tickles his
(shs)nose.

O
an
and
a
wand

_____
_____
_____

er,

...

Oldishmabianman
haulsaredriftedan
danas(S)sof
theofoftheoffofano
wt;

but a

(Look, Purple
Martin, it is a

Nowt Ball, never
thought

to be an a

ae

aeyp....

Look, look, Purple   for ...
Martin, it is ah it
is a   must not;
old
Cat that appears   must not;
(that & which)
now and now a   must not;
gain,   must not;
now   must not;
ythenly   must not;

as an never to be
nowt   must not!

Ball.   Man-haul no
                                       sensitive planz,

Oh beg thys
question   na na na
old
                                       nor unfurl
Cat as an Eth [Ð   mabinogian
                                            no no no.

foretold;
                                       ~

High as a squ
mountain shoe of
a

lace not
connected to
the
yblue berried diet;
oh, to the
savagest true
sage in full

blozzom,
moun(n)tain
burrow(w)ing to
under
and go de(e)ep
under a thee

walkway all down:

down, down –

down ...

~

The Getulis

whoarethe?

(All things
fal(l)ing in a ...

aether, an

ae;

dropped in aether
fall; adest;

as
you,

you, ah,

are

~

Sage, sagest
suggest of blue
to, of a a

peri

winkle;

be loo;
of a blew.
    (Who are
there, Lou?

15.
☉ House of nails &
o moths;
and in
error
never at all what
the what was;

was a cruelty
mishandled,
ganched, and
splatched, and
bare-knuckled;
an old
sheer cat, fool at
the

gander pull in
Poor England;
o,
an out enough in
& out of
all down counts,
for all to see,
dumbed
up and
both down for a
full count, if
only the countless
one, a

riddle sublime of

fixed rate

accrual

an
never;

never to a bee

stung by a
perhaps a be

own

catta.

Back from there.
The far.

To here's empty
now.
A start of Time

stilled, stationary,

you can

hear a voice not

calling to say.

(hello)

Her eyes all
unanswered
questions.

The now, latched.

(hatched)

~

And and so does
in true, in
thrush
of a true, true
deed
court the,

the almost above
as it wanders,
bootless
below, so below
the,
witness
asphalt on a
surd
line, slow;

so slow a surd as
to almost be.

———

Connoitre thus:
the remnant
shoe
walks as though
all wits
were
called to answer
for an omen's
reck.

This is so. Reck.
To blithe
and
un button

all hempen
portal

locks. Be brave,
you who go

to the, full
in fatal absences.

Replete with an or
and an and.

Zero fetching a
dime-bag
drama.

Leave your surd
dream above

or below
the,

the feet of the
just, for it is only
they that,

that they do not
matter much, to

(too).

~

o red mouse, red

mouse red

mouse o

~

The(e) Red Sun's
big & golly:

Insurrect that, my
sleepy
creature, partner
in the pluckery
of time;

Nowt's all, naft. A
Raddle-riddle drift
a
due....

Dawn is an idle
cat sometime
        some
where
else o ah
cattatta;
else o ah
cattatta

(Ball of a solar)

as though the the
belonged to the

he whom

the one whom
bore no

the ball with and
without
a
a, er, an
a:

a ball without a
pedal break.

~

o (oh) zero;

And an o of If(f)s.

16.
Awe

St
er
n

  Moon dip
moon dip mmood
dog
    break a plate
break a plate
        howl a
broken plate
Howl a moon

Going on the boo
line, with great
stuff, o,
o, all
else dreadled;

as of a flare

as of a fire stare

as of a born blip

as of a nard
(smutch'd or
nay);

as of a rune

as of an *ae*:

Moko miro
Moko miro
Moko miro

Aew

        La
        nd

17.

ᴄAn nihil, an never,
an no
does to
do, and
does the charley
horse

to
a

a degree not
brown-studied

as doctorial
commission
wood

in the Park of
Sparkle, dust
un

pre
drab
and thereby
parked, correctly,
by the nose.

But she is close.

Closer that hit off

82

when
she

did all that chew.
Life's

a

kidney-shaped
door latch that is,
uncannily,
from
once within
thus
judged to be
locked.
Judged by the
unlucky
unlockety,
clueless. For

out there above
the park

is a starched
haze;

sparkle, as of

thee

devils falling all
the flame
here,

and Thor

Clear to
Flatbush....

~

Thor and Snowth
is the question
Ruined
Time
didst call to Catta

and snip out
paper holes
with
an inch
of whose life;

Whose?

Who's a shoe dud
and did fail to be
a
stone
on condition of
doubt?

Whose?

Who is wise to the
why that is
so, so
hidden

behind the

Sibyl
Cat singing –

Bron ton bron ton
bronta ton
      tonka ton?

All measurement
must be rider to
the
same
frozen rope;

For Rome
inkeeps her old
owled eld carpets
in a

room.

In order for there
to be

Room for all

If(f)s.   ...

All a   tail
just   house (horse)
an a
er   Flies; no
an
ear nest of other   puff can out dart
glows   the veil
                                 the,
gloves   ah
and   ...

shows.   Ur vast

~   erptide runnel
                                 infects like
Dust flickers   the,
where (no) wind
lists;   a
                                 a
Scurious as the   ah
softness of cotton   a
                                 termite in amber,

all men

is the cloven hoof.

~

As

_____

_____

Ear nests awe's
wand, to

no
good
end to end & Y ...

As Gizmo sits
most quiet upon
his
pillow;

ear nest to the

music of
a
Lark Ascending

~

In the Dim &
Distant Past
Nothing
    Wayland was
by Anyone

Wayland
Wayland
Wayland

The spuggies are
fledged.